The Science of Living Things

What is an Amphibian?

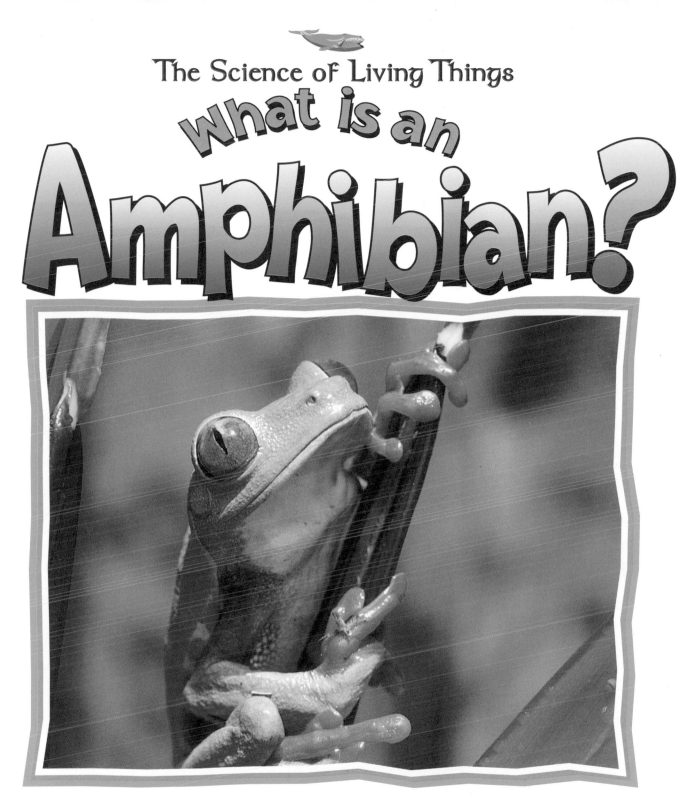

Bobbie Kalman & Jacqueline Langille

Crabtree Publishing Company

The Science of Living Things Series
A Bobbie Kalman Book

To Jan Matthews,
colleague and friend

Editor-in-Chief
Bobbie Kalman

Writing team
Bobbie Kalman
Jacqueline Langille

Managing editor
Lynda Hale

Project editor
John Crossingham

Editing team
Niki Walker
Heather Levigne
Hannelore Sotzek

Copy editor
Kate Calder

Computer design
Lynda Hale
Trevor Morgan (cover type)

**Production coordinator
and photo researcher**
Hannelore Sotzek

Special thanks to
Michael Banelopoulos

Consultant
Joseph T. Collins, Director, The Center for North American
Amphibians and Reptiles (CNAAR)

Photographs
David M. Dennis/Tom Stack & Associates: pages 11 (both),
21 (bottom), 23 (bottom), 26; Eyewire, Inc.: page 18; Bobbie
Kalman: page 3; Kitchin & Hurst/Tom Stack & Associates:
page 4; David Liebman: pages 12, 14, 17 (bottom); Diane
Majumdar: page 31; Robert McCaw: pages 5 (bottom), 8;
Joe McDonald/Tom Stack & Associates: page 17 (top); Photo
Researchers, Inc./Stephen Dalton: pages 9, 20; Rod Planck/
Tom Stack & Associates: page 10; Roger Rageot/David Liebman:
pages 16, 24, 28 (top); Allen Blake Sheldon: pages 5 (top), 19,
23 (top), 27, 30; Tom Stack/Tom Stack & Associates: page 22;
Michael Turco: front cover, title page, pages 13, 21 (top),
28 (bottom), 29

Illustrations
Barbara Bedell: pages 8-9, 15, 20, 26, 31
Bonna Rouse: back cover, pages 6-7, 22, 25

Crabtree Publishing Company

PMB 16A	360 York Road	73 Lime Walk
350 Fifth Avenue,	RR 4	Headington,
Suite 3308	Niagara-on-the-Lake,	Oxford
New York, NY	Ontario, Canada	OX3 7AD
10118	L0S 1J0	United Kingdom

Cataloging in Publication Data
Kalman, Bobbie
    What is an amphibian?

(The science of living things)
Includes index.

ISBN 0-86505-934-9 (library bound) ISBN 0-86505-952-7 (pbk.)
This book introduces various kinds of amphibians, describing their
physiology, behavior, habitats, and life cycles.

1. Amphibians—Juvenile literature. [1. Amphibians.] I. Langille, Jacqueline.
II. Title. III. Series: Kalman, Bobbie. Science of living things.

QL644.2.K34 1999   j597.8   LC 99-25849
                                                CIP

Contents

What is an amphibian? 4

The amphibian family tree 6

An amphibian's life cycle 8

Amphibian bodies 10

Super skin 12

Using their senses 14

Hunters and hunted 16

At home 18

Frogs and toads 20

Salamanders 22

Caecilians 25

Finding a mate 26

Parenting 28

Disappearing amphibians 30

Words to know & Index 32

What is an amphibian?

The word "amphibian" comes from the Latin word *amphibia*, which means "both lives." Amphibians are the only animals that live underwater for the first part of their life but can live on land after they mature. This animal group includes frogs, salamanders, and caecilians. Amphibians are found in every part of the world except in salt water and on the continent of Antarctica.

All amphibians are **cold-blooded**. Reptiles and fish are also cold-blooded animals. The body temperature of a cold-blooded animal does not stay **constant**, or the same most of the time. The animal is as warm or cold as the air or water around it. When an amphibian is too cold, it sits in the sun for a short time. If an amphibian gets too hot, it finds a shady place to cool its body.

Most amphibians, such as this bullfrog, live in cool places. They rest during the day and come out at night.

The first on land

Many scientists think that life on Earth began in the oceans. About 360 million years ago, some types of fish developed lungs for breathing air and bony fins for moving on land. These animals were the ancestors of the first land-dwelling creatures—amphibians.

Amphibians **evolved**, or changed over a long period of time. The body of adult amphibians became well suited to living on land, even though amphibians still live in the water some or all of the time.

Amphibians such as this Chinese dwarf newt can escape underwater enemies by moving onto land.

The legs of this young frog have grown large enough to allow it to walk on land for the first time.

The amphibian family tree

There are over 4500 types of amphibians. They are divided into three **orders**, or groups. Frogs make up the order *Anura*; salamanders belong to the order *Caudata*. The order *Gymnophiona* is made up of legless amphibians called caecilians.

Gymnophiona

Caecilians are the only members of the order *Gymnophiona*. There are about 160 types of caecilians. They resemble small snakes without scales. The word *gymnophiona* means "naked snakes."

Anura

The word *anura* means "no tail." Adult members of the order *Anura* do not have a tail. There are about 4000 **species**, or types, of anurans, or frogs. Toads are a type of frog.

(left) The cane toad is the world's largest toad. It lives in more places on Earth than any other amphibian.

(below) Poison-dart frogs live in tropical rain forests.

Caudata

The word *caudata* means "with a tail." There are about 350 species in the order *Caudata*. All caudates are different types of salamanders.

(*above*) A fire salamander lets out a tiny squeal when it is frightened or excited.

(*above*) Newts are the only salamanders that have rough, bumpy skin.

(*right*) A mudpuppy's spotted brown skin allows it to blend in with a muddy river bottom.

(*above*) Sirens, such as this dwarf siren, do not have hind legs. They live only in North America.

(*below*) The three-toed amphiuma lives its whole life underwater.

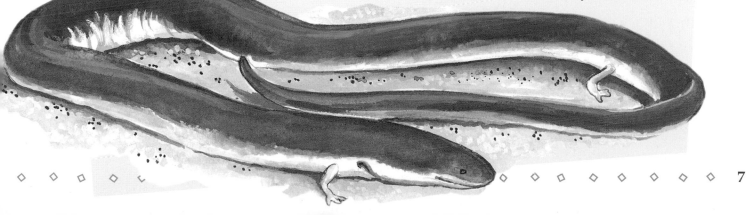

An amphibian's life cycle

Every living thing has a **life cycle**. The stages a creature undergoes between its birth and the time it becomes an adult make up its life cycle. All living things grow and change during their life cycle. An amphibian's life cycle has three stages—**egg**, **larva**, and **adult**. The illustrations across these two pages show the life cycle of a salamander.

1. The **egg** is the first stage of the life cycle. The baby amphibian growing inside the egg is called an **embryo**. Some embryos grow so quickly that they hatch a few days after the egg is laid.

2. When the embryo hatches, it is called a **larva**. Most amphibian **larvae**, or more than one larva, look different from their parents. They have a tail, but they do not have legs. They breathe underwater using **gills**.

(above) The bullfrog remains a **tadpole** for two to three years before becoming an adult.

As it grows, the larva begins ***metamorphosis***. *Metamorphosis is the change from one form into another. The larva starts to grow limbs, and its gills slowly shrink.*

I'm never growing up!

The axolotl, shown right, is a salamander that does not change fully into adult form. This lack of change is called **neoteny**. The axolotl does not have the **hormone** that helps other amphibians change from larvae into adults. Instead, the axolotl stays in the water and keeps its gills for its entire life. Scientists have discovered that when an axolotl is given the missing hormone, it grows into an animal similar to an adult tiger salamander.

The larva continues to grow and change until it looks similar to its parents. In most amphibians, the larva's gills disappear and are replaced by lungs. The larva begins to explore on land.

3. Gradually the amphibian's body develops fully, and the animal leaves the water to live on land. Most amphibians grow into adults within a year. At that time, they are ready to start the life cycle all over again with new eggs.

9

Amphibian bodies

Amphibians are part of a larger animal group called **vertebrates**. Vertebrates are animals that have a backbone. Reptiles, birds, mammals, and fish are also vertebrates. Unlike other vertebrates, an amphibian's skin is bare. It has no fur, hair, feathers, or scales.

Frogs (anurans)

Frogs have hind legs that are longer than their front legs.

Most frogs have large, bulging eyes on top of their head. They use them to look for food and spot dangers.

Frogs have a large mouth. Instead of chewing, they swallow their food whole.

Most frogs have **webs**, or thin flaps of skin, between their toes. Frogs need webbed feet for swimming.

Frogs have large, round ears which are covered by a thin layer of skin called a **tympanum**.

Salamanders (caudates)

A salamander has four toes on its front feet and five toes on its hind feet. Like frogs, some salamanders have webbed toes.

Most salamanders have skin that is smooth and shiny.

Some salamanders have a tail that is slightly flattened. Many newts have a tail like a paddle, which helps them swim through the water.

Salamanders have short legs, but they can run quickly and jump out of the way when they are in danger.

Caecilians (gymnophionans)

Some adult caecilians' eyes are protected by a bony covering or a layer of skin.

A feeler near each nostril is used for finding food.

Caecilians have rings along their body that make them resemble worms.

Super skin

This eastern newt is **shedding** its skin. An amphibian's skin does not grow as the animal gets bigger. Instead, the skin peels off when a new layer has grown underneath. Many amphibians eat the skin they have shed.

All animals must have **oxygen** in order to survive. Many amphibians get the oxygen their body needs by breathing in air through their nostrils. Others take it in through their skin. All amphibians have **porous** skin, which means it has many **pores**, or tiny holes. Oxygen passes through the pores and into the animal's blood, which carries the oxygen throughout the amphibian's body. Some adult lungless salamanders never grow lungs—they breathe only through their skin!

A slimy coat

Most amphibians help keep their skin healthy with a moist layer called **mucus**, or slime. This coating also helps protect them from **predators**, which find it difficult to hold onto an amphibian's slippery body.

Don't touch me!

Some amphibians have skin that **secretes**, or gives off, a poison. The poison often has a bad taste and smell. If a predator bites into one of these amphibians, it gets a terrible taste in its mouth and releases the animal.

The bright patterns on a poison-dart frog's body warn predators that it is poisonous and should be left alone. These tiny frogs have enough poison in them to kill several large animals—including humans!

Using their senses

Most amphibians have five senses—sight, touch, smell, taste, and hearing. Caecilians and some salamanders cannot hear, however. Amphibians use their senses to find food, choose a place to live, and detect enemies.

Seeing is believing

Some amphibians rely on their sight for hunting. They see moving objects better than still ones, so their **prey**, or the animal they hunt for food, is usually safe if it remains still.

What's that smell?

Many types of amphibians live in dark surroundings. When they are underground or in murky water, they rely on their sense of smell to find prey. Smell also helps amphibians identify their mate and find a good home.

Most amphibians have an extra eyelid to cover and protect their eyes underwater and while the animal is jumping or sleeping.

Some amphibians do not breathe air with their nostrils as humans do, but they do use their nostrils for smelling.

Savor the flavor

All amphibians have **taste buds** on their tongue. Taste buds send flavor messages to an animal's brain. When an amphibian has captured its prey, it uses its senses of taste and smell to find out whether or not its catch is **toxic**, or harmful. If the prey tastes good, the amphibian can eat it safely.

When sound waves hit a frog's tympanum, they cause it to vibrate. The frog's brain turns the vibrations into sounds.

Do you hear what I hear?

Most amphibians use hearing to sense predators that are coming toward them. Many also use hearing to find a mate. Frogs and toads use noises such as croaking or peeping to attract mates.

Lines of sense organs

An amphibian's skin is very sensitive. In the water, the animal's **lateral line** organs sense vibrations and changes in water pressure. The organs send messages to the amphibian's brain and let it know if it is close to plants or creatures.

Underwater amphibians, such as this mudpuppy, have lateral line organs along each side of their body. The organs (shown here as black dots) help the animal sense what is in the water around it.

lateral line

Hunters and hunted

All adult amphibians are **carnivores**. Carnivores eat other animals. They eat any live animal that they can swallow, including insects, spiders, snails, slugs, and earthworms. Frogs have especially large appetites. Large frogs sometimes eat mice, rats, small birds, and even small frogs!

A flick of the tongue

Most frogs have a long, sticky tongue for catching small prey. When a frog spots an insect, it flicks out its tongue, grabs the insect, and pulls it into its mouth. This movement happens so quickly that the insect cannot move out of the way to escape.

Frogs such as this Cuban treefrog often use their front limbs to shove their prey into their mouth.

Common prey

Many animals eat amphibians. In fact, some snakes eat only frogs. Fish eat many amphibian eggs and larvae. Amphibians also have a hard time avoiding birds, which attack from the air. Sometimes an amphibian's poison kills its predator, but even an amphibian with a strong poison is not always safe. Some animals such as snakes are **immune** to certain amphibian poisons. The poisons do not hurt them.

To protect themselves from enemies, some salamanders wave their tail in the air. When a predator grabs it, the tail breaks off and the salamander escapes. A new tail grows to replace the old one.

At home

Amphibians live in different **habitats** all over the world. A habitat is the natural place where plants and animals live. **Aquatic** amphibians live in or near rivers, lakes, ponds, swamps, and damp caves. **Terrestrial** amphibians live in forests, deserts, and on mountains.

Most amphibians have a **home range**. A home range is the territory in which an animal lives and finds food. An amphibian knows its home range well. It learns the best places to look for food.

It also learns which predators live nearby and finds safe areas to escape from its natural enemies.

Aquatic amphibians usually hide among water plants when they need a place to rest. Terrestrial amphibians, however, need a safe, moist home. Some dig into leaves on the forest floor or hide under a rotting log. Others take shelter in an abandoned **burrow**, or hole. A few types of amphibians dig their own burrow.

Surviving a drought

Sometimes a **drought** occurs, which means all the water in an area dries up. Amphibians often die during a drought, but some can adapt to dry conditions. Their body forms a mucus coating that hardens into a shell around the animal. This shell traps moisture inside the animal's body until it rains again.

Sleeping all winter

Some amphibians live in areas with cold winters. To keep from freezing, they dig into the bottom of a pond or find a deep hiding place among tree roots. During the winter, their body goes into a type of deep sleep called **hibernation**. They awaken and climb out of their hiding place in the spring.

This white-spotted slimy salamander is emerging from its burrow. Many frogs and salamanders dig a burrow in the ground. Burrows provide a place to escape predators and a spot to cool off when it gets hot.

Frogs and toads

(top) If a frog is startled or afraid, it uses its large, strong legs to hop away quickly. This common frog senses danger and jumps into its favorite pond for safety.

Adult frogs are the leapers and hoppers of the amphibian world. Frogs have long, strong back legs that allow them to take huge leaps. A frog's legs also make excellent flippers for swimming. A toad's back legs are not as long as a frog's, so toads take smaller hops. Certain types of toads walk or run when they are moving around.

Climbers and flyers

Treefrogs spend most of their life above the ground. Their long toes and sticky **toe pads** allow them to climb up tree trunks, hang onto thin branches, and cling to the underside of leaves. Flying treefrogs can jump great distances, but they do not actually fly. The toes on their feet have extra-large webs. Flying treefrogs use this webbing to glide through the air as they jump from tree to tree.

Arboreal, *or tree-dwelling, frogs have eyes that can rotate farther forward than those of other frogs and toads. This movement helps these frogs see directly ahead and below them when they are above ground.*

What is a toad?

A toad is a type of frog. Here are some important toad features:

- Toads are toothless
- Toads have dry skin with bumps called **warts**
- Toads have shorter hind legs than other frogs
- Toads are less active than other types of anurans

(right) Toads are almost always hungry! After a spider is caught by this southern toad's sticky tongue, it has little chance of escaping.

Salamanders

Most adult salamanders are terrestrial and spend their time silently roaming the land. Many are **nocturnal**, which means they are active mainly at night. Coming out at night allows these amphibians to avoid being seen by many predators.

Smooth walkers

A terrestrial salamander's front and back legs are positioned far apart from one another. When it walks, this amphibian bends its body from side to side to allow each foot to move as far ahead as possible. This movement causes a terrestrial salamander's body to twist into an S-shape.

*Some salamanders and newts have a brightly colored belly to warn enemies that they are poisonous. If attacked, these amphibians lift up their head and tail to show their underside. This movement is called the **unken reflex**.*

Underwater living

Sirens, mudpuppies, and amphiumas are aquatic salamanders. They have different bodies and ways of breathing than those of their terrestrial cousins. Sirens have a long body, tiny front legs, and no hind legs. Sirens and mudpuppies breathe underwater using feathery gills. Amphiumas breathe through single, circular gill openings on the sides of their head. Large aquatic amphibians such as giant salamanders take in oxygen through baggy skin. The folds of skin on their body give these amphibians more skin area through which they can breathe.

*Some newts have an extra stage in their life cycle called an **eft**. This eastern newt eft will live on land for several years before returning to the water as an adult.*

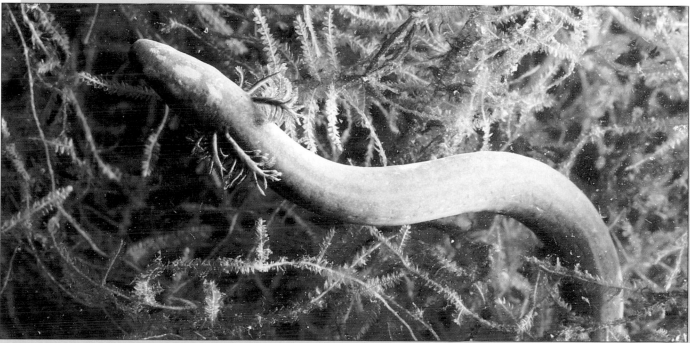

Sirens such as this dwarf siren swim through the water by waving their long body in snakelike motions.

Caecilians

Scientists know little about caecilians because most of these amphibians live underground. Even those caecilians that live underwater are difficult to find. Although caecilians have moist, porous skin, these animals are quite different from other amphibians.

Terrestrial caecilians give birth to young that look like tiny adults. Aquatic caecilians lay eggs and their larvae go through the process of metamorphosis.

Above the ground

Caecilians live in the **tropics**. They come above ground only after heavy rains have flooded the soil. When caecilians travel over the ground, they **slither**, or bend from side to side, in the same way that snakes move. Caecilians can find insects to eat on the ground, but they have few defenses against predators. It is far safer for them to live underground.

Happy burrowing

Caecilians are excellent **burrowers**, or diggers. Underground, they use their hard head and strong muscles to push themselves through damp soil and mud. Since their eyes are not needed in the underground darkness, caecilians are almost blind. Two **sensory tentacles** let them know where they are and help them find prey.

Scientists believe that a caecilian uses its sensory tentacles to taste and smell its surroundings.

eye

sensory tentacle

nostril

Finding a mate

Many amphibians spend most of their life alone. Every spring or summer, however, males and females search for a partner in order to **breed**, or make babies. To find the right mate, many species gather in large groups at ponds and other watery places called **breeding sites**.

I know where I'm going!

An amphibian's breeding site is usually the same place where it was born. Even if it lives a long distance from its breeding site, it returns there by **instinct**, which means it knows how to get there without being taught.

(below) During courtship a male eastern newt often grabs hold of the female with its hind legs.

Look at me!

Amphibian males show off their talents to win a partner. Salamanders perform a **courting dance**. The males move their body in special ways to prove to a female that they are the best mate in the area. Some males wave their tail or limbs to get a female's attention. Others stroke a female's head with their head.

Sing, sing a song

Most frogs use their voice to attract a female or scare away other males. To make a **mating call**, the males blow up a pouch of skin on their throat called a **vocal sac**, as shown above. Air moving inside the vocal sac makes a croaking or peeping noise. The males "sing" without opening their mouth.

Dusky salamanders lay their eggs under a rock or in a rotting log. The mother curls around her clutch to protect it and keep it moist until the babies hatch.

Many poison-dart frogs lay eggs on land. The male waits until the eggs hatch and then carries the larvae on his back as they grow into tadpoles.

Parenting

Amphibians lay their eggs in moist places such as in water or beneath a log. The eggs do not have a hard shell—they have a jelly coating for protection. Eggs must remain moist or the embryos inside will die.

How many eggs?

Some amphibians lay their eggs one at a time, carefully hiding them from predators. Most, however, lay a batch of eggs called a **clutch**. A small clutch has only five eggs, but many have more than 10,000. Some amphibians lay as many as 30,000 eggs when they breed!

Parents and guardians

Amphibians that have a large number of eggs often leave them alone after they are laid. Although predators may eat some of the eggs, many do hatch. Amphibians that lay only a few eggs at a time often stay close to their eggs to protect them from predators.

Some amphibians stay with their young in order to help them learn to survive. This red-eyed treefrog mother is giving a guided tour to her **froglet**, or young frog.

Words to know

acid rain Rain that contains pollution

adapt To become different to suit a new environment

aquatic Describing a living thing that lives in, on, or near water

burrow (n) An animal's underground home; (v) to dig underground

carnivore An animal that eats mainly meat

cold-blooded Describing an animal whose body temperature changes with the temperature of its surroundings

eft The third, land-based stage in the life cycle of some newts

food chain A pattern of eating and being eaten

gills The organs an aquatic animal uses to breathe oxygen from water

hibernation A winter sleep during which an animal's heart and breathing rates slow down and its body temperature drops to near freezing

hormone A substance produced by an animal to help it grow

immune Unable to be harmed by a poison

instinct Knowledge of how to do something without being taught

lungs The organs an animal uses to breathe oxygen from air

oxygen A gas that animals must breathe in order to survive

predator An animal that hunts and eats other animals

rain forest A forest that receives over 80 inches (200 cm) of rain a year

sensory tentacles Organs on a caecilian's head that are used to taste and smell

tadpole The larva of a frog

taste buds Tiny organs on an animal's tongue that sense the taste of an object

terrestrial Describing a living thing that lives on land

tropics An area with a hot, wet climate

tympanum A frog's outer eardrum

vocal sac A large pouch of skin which frogs fill with air to make sounds

wetland An area that has waterlogged soil

Index

adult 5, 6, 8, 9, 11, 12, 16, 20, 22, 23, 25

amphiumas 7, 23

birds 10, 16, 17

body 4, 5, 9, 10-11, 12, 13, 15, 19, 22, 23, 27, 30

breathing 5, 8, 12, 14, 23

caecilians 4, 6, 11, 14, 24-25

ears 10, 15

eggs 8, 9, 17, 25, 28

enemies 5, 13, 14, 17, 18, 19, 22, 25, 28

eyes 10, 11, 14, 21, 25, 29

food 10, 11, 14, 15, 16, 18, 25, 31

frogs 4, 5, 6, 8, 10, 11, 13, 15, 16, 17, 18, 19, 20-21, 27, 28, 29, 30

gills 8, 9, 23

home 14, 18-19, 30

insects 16, 25, 31

land 4, 5, 9, 22, 23, 28

larva 8, 9, 17, 25, 28, 31

legs 5, 6, 7, 8, 10, 11, 20, 21, 22, 23, 26

lungs 5, 9, 12

mate 14, 15, 26-27

metamorphosis 8, 25

mouth 10, 13, 15, 16, 21, 27

mudpuppies 7, 15, 23

newts 5, 7, 11, 12, 22, 23, 26

poison 6, 13, 17, 22, 28, 30

pollution 30, 31

salamanders 4, 6, 7, 8, 9, 11, 12, 14, 17, 19, 22-23, 27, 28, 30

sirens 7, 23

skin 7, 10, 11, 12-13, 15, 21, 23, 25, 27

tadpole 8, 28

tail 6, 7, 8, 11, 17, 22, 27

toads 6, 15, 20-21, 31

tongue 15, 16, 21

water 4, 5, 7, 8, 9, 11, 14, 15, 18, 19, 20, 23, 25, 26, 28, 30, 31

1 2 3 4 5 6 7 8 9 0   Printed in the U.S.A.   8 7 6 5 4 3 2 1 0 9